BICYCLES

BICYCLES

BY PATRICIA LAKIN

ALADDIN

New York   London   Toronto   Sydney   New Delhi

For my dad, Samuel Miller Lakin, who
lovingly taught me to ride a two-wheeler

ALADDIN

An imprint of Simon & Schuster Children's Publishing Division

1230 Avenue of the Americas, New York, New York 10020

First Aladdin hardcover edition February 2017

Text copyright © 2017 by Simon & Schuster, Inc.

Cover photograph of bicycle copyright © 2017 by Aaron Dykstra

All other cover photographs and illustrations copyright © Thinkstock

Photographs of bicycles on pages 2 and 3, and featured photographs on pages 9, 11, 12, 14, 15, 16, 17, 18,

19, 20, 21, 22, 23, 24, and 25 copyright © 2017 by Aaron Dykstra

Black-and-white photographs on pages 8, 29 (at left), and 30 courtesy of the Library of Congress

Photograph of locomotive on page 13 copyright © 1992 by James G. Howes

Photograph of woman and vintage bicycle on page 29 (at right) copyright © Shutterstock

All other interior photographs and illustrations copyright © Thinkstock

The Making Foundation logo courtesy of the Making Foundation.

For information about special discounts for bulk purchases, please contact Simon & Schuster
Special Sales at 1-866-506-1949 or business@simonandschuster.com.

The Simon & Schuster Speakers Bureau can bring authors to your live event.

For more information or to book an event, contact the Simon & Schuster Speakers Bureau at
1-866-248-3049 or visit our website at www.simonspeakers.com.

Book designed by Lissi Erwin / SPLENDID CORP.

The text of this book was set in Univers LTD, Haneda, and AG Book Stencil.

Manufactured in China 1116 SCP

10 9 8 7 6 5 4 3 2 1

Library of Congress Cataloging-in-Publication Data

Names: Lakin, Patricia, 1944– author.

Title: Bicycles / Patricia Lakin.

Description: New York : Aladdin, 2017. | Series: Made by hand ; 2

Identifiers: LCCN 2016034643 | ISBN 9781481478960 (paper over board) |
    ISBN 9781481478977 (eBook)

Subjects: LCSH: Bicycles—Juvenile literature. | Bicycles—Design and
    construction—Juvenile literature. | BISAC: JUVENILE NONFICTION /
    Technology / How Things Work-Are Made. | JUVENILE NONFICTION / Technology /
Machinery & Tools. | JUVENILE NONFICTION / Crafts & Hobbies.

Classification: LCC TL412 .L35 2017 | DDC 629.227/2—dc23

LC record available at https://lccn.loc.gov/2016034643

GRAB THE HANDLEBARS!

HOP ON!

PEDAL HARD!

SPEED **away.**

YOU'RE RIDING A BIKE.

It's your ticket to travel. Near or far, with pedal power a bike will get you almost anywhere.

Ever wonder how the bicycle came to be? In the following pages you'll find out. You'll also get a behind-the-scenes look at a special company where bicycles are *made by hand*. You'll discover how the man who created this business just had to use his hands to make an object he loves—the bicycle.

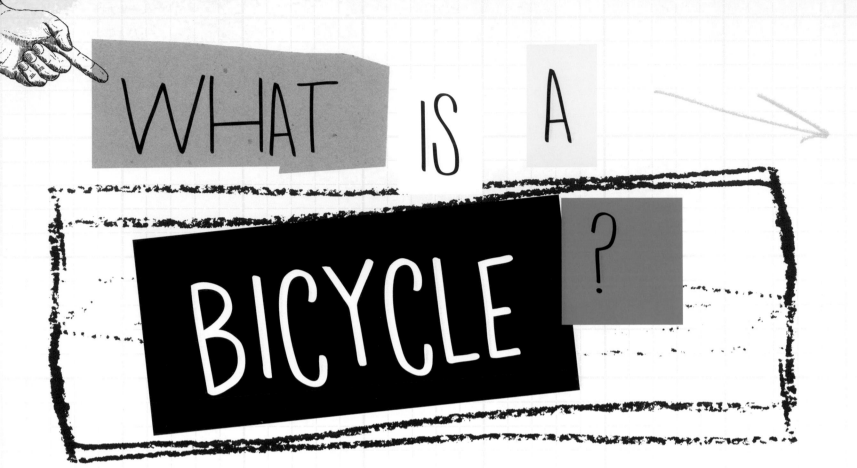

WHAT IS A BICYCLE?

WHEEL

THE HEART OF A BICYCLE is a double-diamond frame made up of two triangle-shaped pieces of metal. Attached to that frame are two wheels, two pedals, a seat, and handlebars. Want the bike to move? Just turn the pedals. That action moves the chain, which is attached to toothed wheels called sprockets. The sprockets are attached to the back wheel. *Whoosh*, you're off! Want to stop? Just put on the brakes!

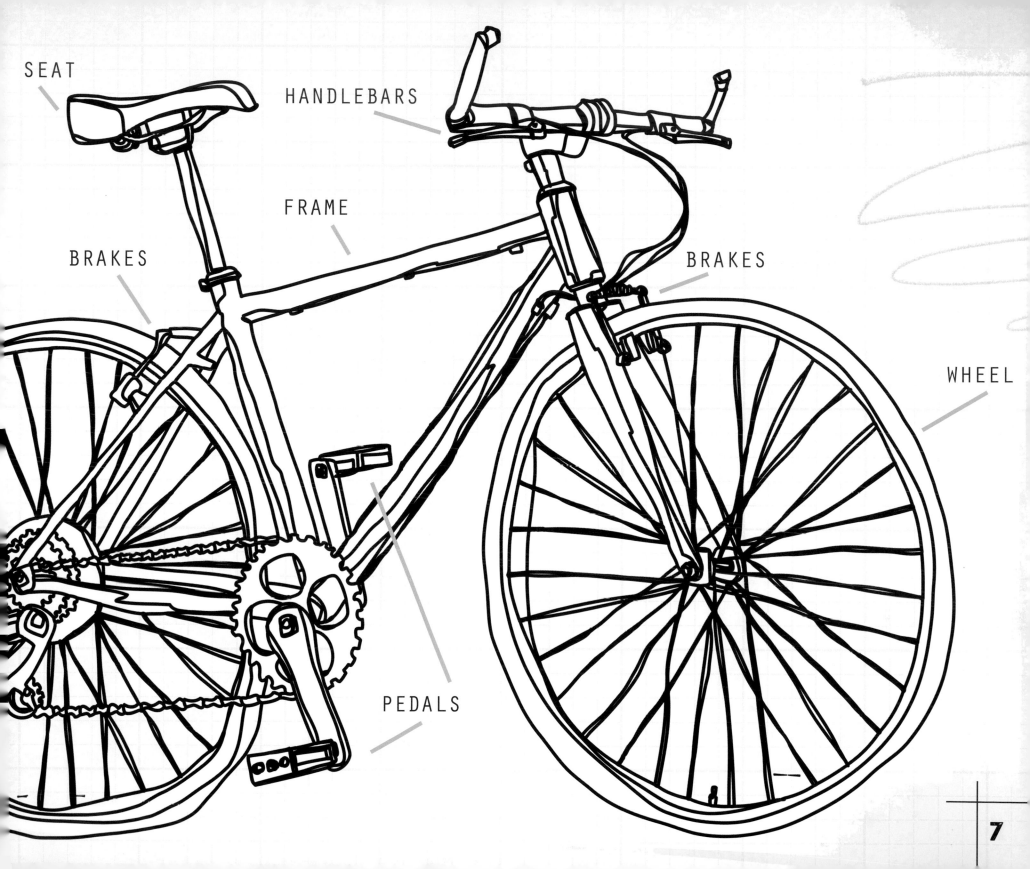

SEAT

HANDLEBARS

FRAME

BRAKES

BRAKES

WHEEL

PEDALS

HISTORY OF THE BICYCLE

IN THE 1800s, if people wanted to travel by land, they walked, rode a horse, or sat in a carriage pulled by a horse. Many wished for a "horseless" carriage.

In 1817, Germany's Baron von Drais built a horseless carriage. It had two wooden wheels that were attached to a straight wooden board. The rider sat on the board and pushed off with one foot at a time. His invention was called the Draisine. Later, one clever person added pedals, but to the front wheel.

By the mid-1800s more builders were making these two-wheeled "mechanical horses." People now called them velocipedes and used them to travel.

In the 1870s, English engineer Henry Lawson developed the Safety Bicycle. He took a long interconnected metal chain and placed it around the hub of the bicycle's rear wheel. The chain also went around a metal sprocket. That sprocket was in front of the rear wheel. Pedals moved the sprocket. The moving chain turned the back wheel. Thanks to Lawson's idea, one push on the pedal moved both wheels!

Soon after, another Englishman, John Kemp Starley, improved on Lawson's design. He created the Rover Safety Bike.

The shape of Starley's bicycle frame hasn't changed much over time. It is still pretty much a diamond-shaped design. And that's where Aaron Dykstra comes in. Ever since he was a young boy, he dreamed of making things. He also loved bicycles. So Aaron found a way to put his two loves together. Today he creates handmade bicycle frames.

MEET AARON DYKSTRA

TAP! TAP! BANG! BANG! Eight-year-old Aaron pretended he was building something in his backyard. He loved making things and wished he could do that in school. Instead he had to sit still all day—and that was tough.

But he could sit for hours listening to his grandparents' travel stories. Years earlier they had explored Europe by bicycle. Aaron loved that their bicycles had given them such freedom to travel! In his mind his grandparents' experiences made bicycles magical.

In high school Aaron had an after-school job at a bike shop and biked to and from work. Before long he was fixing bikes at the shop.

Aaron knew bikes *had* to be part of his life. But how?

After high school Aaron joined the United States Air Force. He worked on jet engines in desert areas in the Middle East. Metal, mechanical parts, and burning heat filled his days. During his time off he sketched his own designs for bicycle frames. That was it! Aaron decided to start a business. He'd make bicycle frames by hand.

In 2007, Aaron married his girlfriend, Michelle, and settled in Roanoke, Virginia. Aaron decided that it was time for him to learn bicycle frame building. He traveled to Colorado to study with world-famous bicycle frame builder Koichi Yamaguchi.

The bicycle frame is like the bike's skeleton: everything attaches to it. On his first day studying with Yamaguchi, Aaron picked up a fiery hot welding torch and began to bind the metal rods of the frame together. Once he got home, Aaron practiced his welding skills for a year. He also made his very own bicycle.

AARON AT EIGHT YEARS OLD

AARON SAWING WOOD AT AGE FIVE.
(NEVER USE A SAW WITHOUT YOUR PARENTS' HELP!)

AARON AND HIS DAUGHTER

Here is what Aaron says:

"TAKE A MOMENT TO APPRECIATE SOMETHING THAT WAS MADE BY HAND. CHANCES ARE THERE IS A STORY BEHIND IT. AND THERE IS A PERSON WHO LOVINGLY BROUGHT THAT OBJECT TO LIFE."

The first time he took it for a ride, he felt such joy. He'd dreamed of this day—when he would make something with his own hands that he could ride. Now he'd done it!

Aaron was ready to start his business. He used a part of his city's history in his company's name. Roanoke is where the last steam locomotive was created and preserved. It was named the 611. People thought the 611 train was the best and most beautifully designed— which was exactly how Aaron wanted his bicycles to be. That is how Six-Eleven Bicycle Co. was born.

THE 611 LOCOMOTIVE

HOW THE BIKE FRAME IS MADE

BEFORE HE BEGAN taking orders to make bicycles for other people, Aaron practiced for more than a year. He made many of his mistakes then. He uses his mistakes as a way to learn.

Today all of Aaron's bicycles are sleek and beautiful. In order to make such a simple machine, he has a workshop that is filled with tables, saws, tubs, and tubes. Aaron's customers ask him to make a bike frame that is just for them. It takes Aaron two weeks to make one of these frames. For many of the steps he uses his hands. For other steps, such as cutting steel tubing, he must use machines.

Step into Aaron's large white-walled workshop, and you'll see metal everywhere! There are seven large metal tables, plus metal cutting machines, metal tools neatly stored, stuffed-full metal shelves, and an assortment of steel tubing. Hanging high up on the wall are steel wheels and finished bike frames.

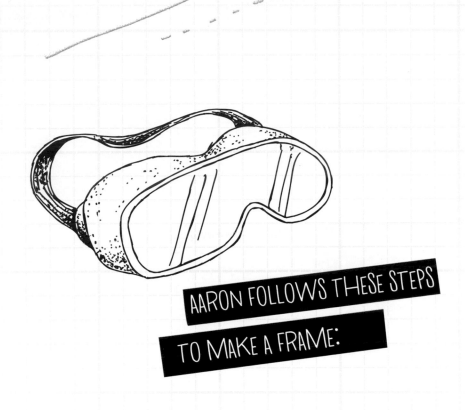

AARON FOLLOWS THESE STEPS TO MAKE A FRAME:

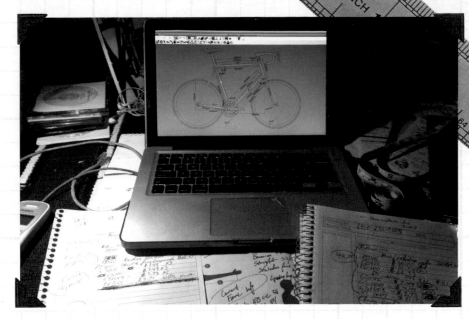

STEP 1: Aaron asks his customer two important questions:
- How will they use their bicycle?
- What are their measurements—height, weight, and leg length?

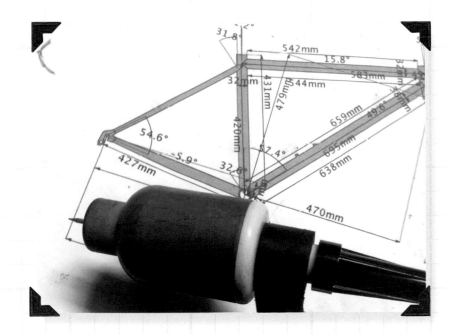

STEP 2: Aaron enters all that information into a computer. He designs the bicycle frame using a software program that gives him a blueprint with the exact measurements for the frame.

STEP 3: After putting on his safety goggles and gloves, Aaron selects the steel tubing he'll use. (The steel he uses is the same kind of steel used to make airplanes!)

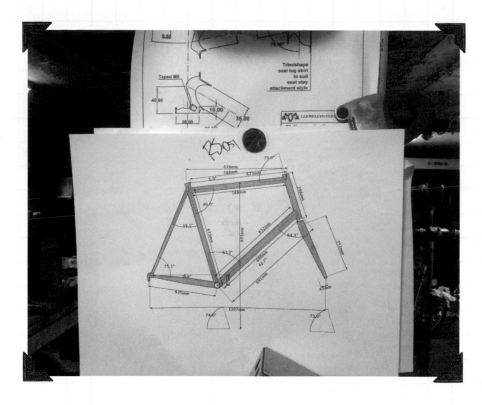

STEP 4: Aaron checks each section of tube to make sure it is straight and has no dents.

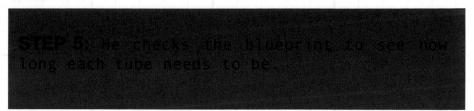

STEP 5: He checks the blueprint to see how long each tube needs to be.

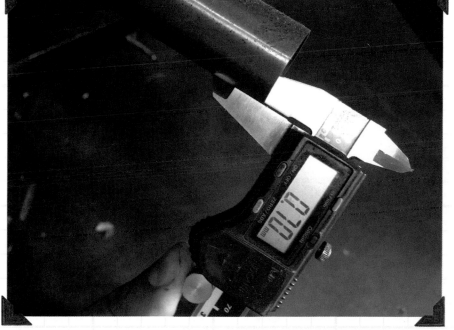

STEP 6: He measures the inside wall of each tube. He uses thick-walled steel tubes for some parts of the frame and thinner-walled tubes for other parts.

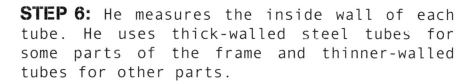

STEP 8: Aaron then uses a hand file to make each cut area smooth.

STEP 7: Aaron uses a special tool called a milling machine to cut the tubes. He cuts some tubes in a straight line. Some he cuts at an angle.

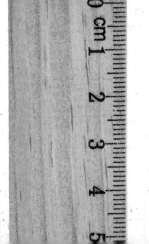

STEP 10: Aaron temporarily tacks the tubes together using tiny welds. (A weld is a kind of "glue" made from melted metal.)

STEP 9: Then he goes to his frame jig. This holds all the pieces together. (Now the steel tubes begin to look like a bicycle frame.)

STEP 11: After he makes those small welds, Aaron can take the frame out of the jig. He puts the frame onto a special table that can hold the temporary structure on both sides. He checks to make sure all the tubes are totally straight.

STEP 13: But first Aaron spreads a special paste over those joint parts. The paste is called flux, and it keeps the metal from getting too hot where the torch will hit.

STEP 12: Now Aaron is ready to weld all the joints together. He uses a flame torch to melt brass, which will hold the joints.

2 CM

AN UP-CLOSE
LOOK AT FLUX!

STEP 15: When the Flux cools, it hardens to be like glass. Aaron puts the bicycle frame into a tub of hot water, which takes off all the Flux.

STEP 14: Aaron removes his goggles and gloves. He puts on special glasses that protect his eyes from the glare of the torch and special gloves that protect his hands from the flame's heat.

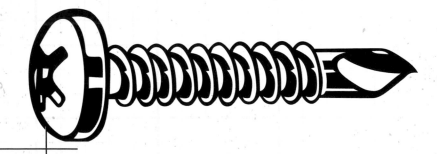

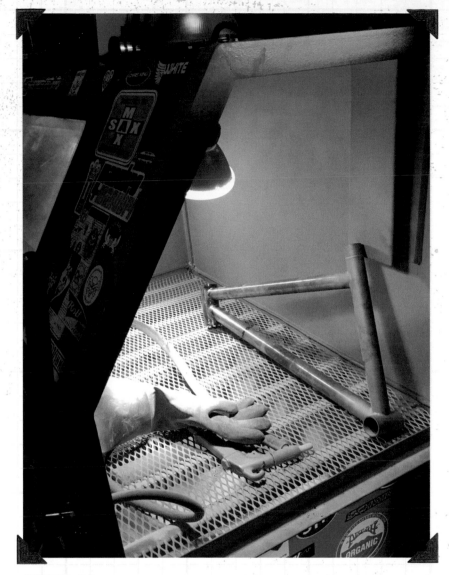

STEP 16: Then Aaron puts the bicycle frame back on his special table to once again make sure that all the parts are straight.

STEP 17: Aaron holds the bike in a vise and begins to hand sand the joints to make sure each one is smooth, so that the bike can be the best—and safest—bike possible.

STEP 18: Then Aaron puts the bicycle frame into a specially made cabinet called a media blaster. It has a window on top. It has side slots with gloves, where Aaron can slip his hands in. He "blasts" the frame with very finely chopped windshield glass. This cleans up the frame if any rust is there. And it prepares the frame for painting.

STEP 19: Aaron sends the frame to a company that paints metal. Aaron tells the painter which color and style his customer wants.

STEP 20: Once the frame is painted, Aaron then adds on all the parts—such as the seat, wheels, gears, pedals, and handlebars.

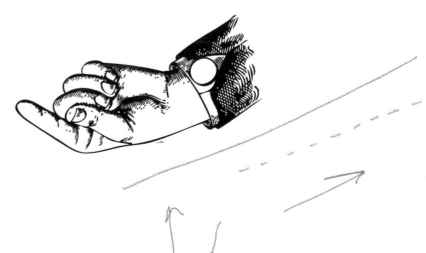

AARON'S HANDMADE BICYCLE
IS NOW READY TO ROLL
OUT OF HIS SHOP AND GO OUT INTO THE WORLD.

NOW IT'S YOUR TURN

The Making Foundation

www.makingfoundation.org

WHEN AARON WAS GROWING UP, he wished someone had told him what he knows today. Making things by hand brings a joy and excitement that is hard to beat. You can make a living doing it and feel empowered.

Aaron's wish led him to create a program for middle school students called The Making Foundation. Its goal is to inspire confidence in kids by teaching them to make things by hand *and* by teaching them to value the skills they learn while doing so. In the process of making objects, they will learn about science, technology, engineering, and mathematics—the STEM subjects.

Want to build something by hand? It can be fun, educational, *and* simple. Create a paper-plate mask, or make a necklace by stringing a shoelace with pasta.

Making things means using your imagination. Imagine making something new from something used. That adds up to creating *and* recycling! Can that used plastic cup become a decorated pencil holder? Can that old sock become a hand puppet? Are your ideas running wild? Good! You'll be using your head and your hands, and recycling in the process.

Recycling even applies to old bicycles. You can get a fixed-up bike that's safe to ride. Or you can learn some bike repair skills and fix bikes. For your efforts, you can "earn" your own bike. Got a bike that you've outgrown? You can donate it to someone who would love to hop on, pedal hard, and speed away!

BICYCLE TIME LINE

1817—Baron Karl von Drais invents the wooden two-wheeled "running machine," or Draisine.

1820–1840s—Carriage makers design horseless carriages, some with three or four wheels.

1845—R. W. Thomson invents an air-filled, or pneumatic, tire.

1865—Pierre Michaux forms a company to sell what he created—a two-wheeler that has pedals on the front wheels. His "mechanical horse" is also nicknamed a "boneshaker."

1868—In the United States and in Europe velocipedes become popular.

1873–4—Englishman Henry Lawson designs a chain-driven rear-wheel bicycle.

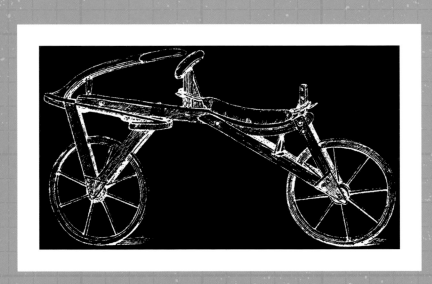

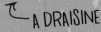

A DRAISINE

1878—An American company, Columbia, begins making two-wheelers, now called bicycles.

1888—John Boyd Dunlop, a Scottish inventor and veterinarian, receives a patent for pneumatic (air-filled) bicycle tires. He had created the tires for his son's tricycle to provide a smoother ride.

1890—Englishman John Kemp Starley designs a bicycle that has a diamond-shaped frame, much like the bicycle frames of today.

1894—The first bicycle path is built in Prospect Park, Brooklyn, New York, and stretches for five and a half miles, to Coney Island on Brooklyn's south shore.

1896—Swiss professor Charles Challand builds a bicycle with a reclining seat. He called it a Normal Bicycle because the rider sat in a more normal position. This recumbent bicycle was also nicknamed the "Easy Chair."

1897—After Challand's design, bicycle makers design their own "Easy Chair" or recumbent bikes. The rider sits on a low seat and leans back to pedal.

EARLY RECUMBENT BICYCLE

1920s—As automobiles become more popular, bicycles are thought to be like toys, only for boys and girls.

1934—Recumbent bicycles are banned from bicycle races because they go so fast.

1967—Davis, California, is the first city in the United States to install a bike lane on a roadway also meant for vehicles.

1970—The first Earth Day is celebrated. People realize the importance of bicycles—that they do not cause pollution and give riders great exercise.

1971—BMX bikes are made to ride off-road and for trick riding.

1978—MIT professor and avid bicyclist David Gordon Wilson designs a recumbent bike called Avatar 1000. It is the first recumbent bicycle in recent times that is produced and offered for sale.

1990—The nonprofit organization Bikes Not Bombs creates a learning-and-earning bicycle program they call Earn-A-Bike. Students learn how to overhaul a bicycle and ride safely, in order to "earn" their own bike. This program inspired similar programs to sprout elsewhere in the United States.

1996—Mountain bike competition becomes part of the Olympic Games, held in Atlanta, Georgia.

2002—There are close to twenty designated bike lanes in cities across the United States.

2014—There are two hundred designated bike lanes in cities across the United States.

2015—Many cities in the United States and around the world have bikes available on the street for sharing or short-term rental.

2016—There are 217 designated bike lanes in 82 cities across the United States. Is your city one of them? Go to www.peopleforbikes.org.

GLOSSARY & RESOURCES

BLUEPRINT: A printed plan for a design.

HUB: The center part of a wheel.

DRAISINE: An early wooden bicycle designed by Baron von Drais.

PNEUMATIC TIRE: A tire filled with air.

SPROCKET: One of many toothlike projections on the rim of a wheel, which connects with the links of a chain and causes it to move.

RECUMBENT: A bicycle designed so the rider pedals with her/his legs out in front while leaning back in a specially designed seat.

SKELETON: The basic frame on which something is built.

VELOCIPEDE: The name given to early versions of bicycles. It comes from Latin and means "quick footed." [*Velocis* means "quick." *Ped* means "footed."]

WELD: To fuse or join two pieces of metal together using high heat.

TOOLS:

MILLING MACHINE: A machine used to drill holes in metal and to cut steel at precise angles.

JIG: A tool or device made to hold an object so that work can be done on that object. A frame jig holds the bicycle frame while it's being worked on.

MEDIA BLASTER: A machine enclosed in a cabinet that rapidly spits out sand or other finely ground materials to remove rust from metal.

VISE: A metal tool with movable jaws that holds a part in place.

BOOKS:

David V. Herlihy, *Bicycle: The History* (New Haven: Yale University Press, 2004).

Editors of *Bicycling* magazine, *The Noblest Invention: An Illustrated History of the Bicycle*. (New York: Rodale, Inc., 2003).

Robert Curley, *The Britannica Guide to Inventions That Changed the Modern World* (New York: Rosen Publishing Group, 2009).

WEBSITES:

www.britannica.com
www.oxforddnb.com
amhistory.si.edu/onthemove/themes/story_69_2.html
www.bicycleman.com/history/history.htm
www.sspiprints.com/image/101139/lawsons-bicyclette-1879
www.gracesguide.co.uk/Harry_Lawson

www.peopleforbikes.org
www.roadswerenotbuiltforcars.com/lawson/
cityofdavis.org/about-davis/history-symbols/first-bicycle-lanes-in-davis
www.lepetitbraquet.fr/chron24_Michaux.html
www.bicyclehistory.net/bicycle-history